NORTHERN KENTUCKY'S
FIRST COLLEGE

NORTHERN KENTUCKY'S FIRST COLLEGE

VILLA MADONNA–THOMAS MORE COLLEGE

RONALD A. MIELECH

Charleston THE History PRESS London

Published by The History Press
Charleston, SC 29403
www.historypress.net

First published 2010

Manufactured in the United States

ISBN 978.1.59629.816.3

Library of Congress CIP data applied for.

CONTENTS

ACKNOWLEDGEMENTS

Sincere thanks to Sister Margaret Stallmeyer, CDP; Dr. Paul Tenkotte, former chairman of the History Department; Kelly Morris, PR director; Monica Ginney, alumni director; Mr. Cory Blackson, PR for athletics; my many, many consultants, too many to begin to mention; the entire faculty and staff of the college; my wife, Nancy, and our son, Stephen, for their incredible patience and help; the library staff, especially Jim McKellog, director, and Joyce McKinley, circulation supervisor; my brother-in-law, Steve Vaal, my personal computer guru; Sister Mary Philip, SND, the former college archivist who saved me countless hours of searching and identifying; and every alum or faculty member whose photograph or name I regretfully was unable to include in this volume.

The entire proceeds from the sale of this book will be donated to the Anne Marie Mielech Creative Writing Scholarship at Thomas More College.

The administration building, Villa Madonna College, 1921.

INTRODUCTION

There has been some mystery surrounding the founding date of Villa Madonna College. We know now that the college was indeed founded in 1921 by the Sisters of Saint Benedict of Covington, primarily to educate the nuns of their order who were teaching in the Catholic schools in the region. New teaching standards in Kentucky required college-level training of all teachers. This left the Sisters of Notre Dame and the Sisters of Divine Providence, whose members were also teaching in area schools, without a local college program.

In 1923, Bishop Francis Howard was appointed to the Diocese of Covington. In 1928, he placed Villa Madonna College under the sponsorship of the diocese. An application for a new state charter would have required the college to conform more closely to the state's view of higher education—a conformity that Bishop Howard, an eminent educator, found unacceptable. So the original charter was used.

THE BEGINNING

The Bishops of Covington Are the Chancellors of the College

Bishop Francis Howard.

Bishop Francis Howard (1923–1944)

Bishop Mulloy (1944–1960)

Bishop Ackerman (1961–1977)

Bishop Hughes (1978–1996)

Bishop Muench (1997–2001)

Bishop Foys (2002–)

Bishop Foys.

The CEOs of the College

Sister Domitilla, OSB.

Sister Domitilla, OSB (1921–1929)

Father Lieck (1929–1943)

Father Corby (1943–1944)

Father McCarty (1945–1949)

Father Aud (1949–1951)
Father Aud was granted a leave of absence from the college in 1951 so he might serve as a chaplain

in the United States Army. He served in Korea. Upon his release from the army, he returned to the area, only to die shortly thereafter of causes unrelated to the war.

Father John Murphy.

Father John Murphy:
Appointed acting dean in 1951
Appointed president in 1956
Made a monsignor in 1962
Retired in 1971
Died August 1, 2001, in car accident on AA Highway

Father Murphy was the youngest college president in the United States. He was twenty-eight years old at the time of his appointment.

His memoirs, *Personal Reflections*, on his years at Villa Madonna–Thomas More College (1951–1971), only available through the college, is an important document.

Presidential appointment.

Father Murphy's Successors

Richard Degraff (1971–1978)

Robert Giroux (1978–1982)

Sister Margaret Stallmeyer, CDP.

Thomas Coffey (1982–1986)

Charles Bensman (1986–1992)

Father William Cleves (1992–2001)

Joseph Lee (2001–2004)

Sister Margaret Stallmeyer, CDP (2004–)

After being placed under the sponsorship of the diocese in 1928, Villa Madonna College turned its attention to academic development. During the summer of 1929, the academic program received prime consideration. It was agreed that each community should be responsible for supplying qualified chairmen for different departments. The staffing of the Education Department was to be shared by the communities.

The eight departments formed in 1929 were chaired as follows:

EDUCATION: Sisters of Divine Providence, Sister M. Callixta
ENGLISH: Sisters of Divine Providence, Sister Mary of the Incarnation
MODERN LANGUAGES: Sisters of Divine Providence, Sister Hilarine
ANCIENT LANGUAGES: Sisters of St. Benedict, Sister Mary Annunciata
MATHEMATICS: Sisters of St. Benedict, Sister Domitilla
HISTORY: Sisters of Notre Dame, Sister Mary Carmelite
SCIENCE: Sisters of Notre Dame, Sister Ignace
PHILOSOPHY: Reverend John Laux

We owe much of our knowledge of the information contained in this book to Sister Irmina Salinger's document, *Retrospect and Vista: The First Fifty Years of Thomas More College.* Sister was a legend—the right hand of all the CEOs of her time; an inspiration and a wonderful person. A woman for all seasons.

Sister Mary Irmina Salinger, OSB, PhD.

WHEN JOHNNY CAME MARCHING HOME

After the college's inception in 1929, classes carried on much as usual until Bishop William Mulloy, newly appointed to the Covington Diocese, announced to the stunned graduates of the class of 1945 that the college would become coeducational the following year.

The college had been made coeducational, as seen in the photo of an advanced Spanish class on the next page. Their reading material commemorated Cervantes's 400th birthday. Unlike Don Quixote, who appeared in the readings, the veterans on hand hadn't been tilting at windmills.

While most classes became coeducational, some, such as the physical education classes seen on page 15, remained distinct.

Graduation with Bishop Mulloy.

Coeducational Spanish class.

In physical education for refined young ladies, girls take graceful exercise in the back of the main building on Twelfth Street.

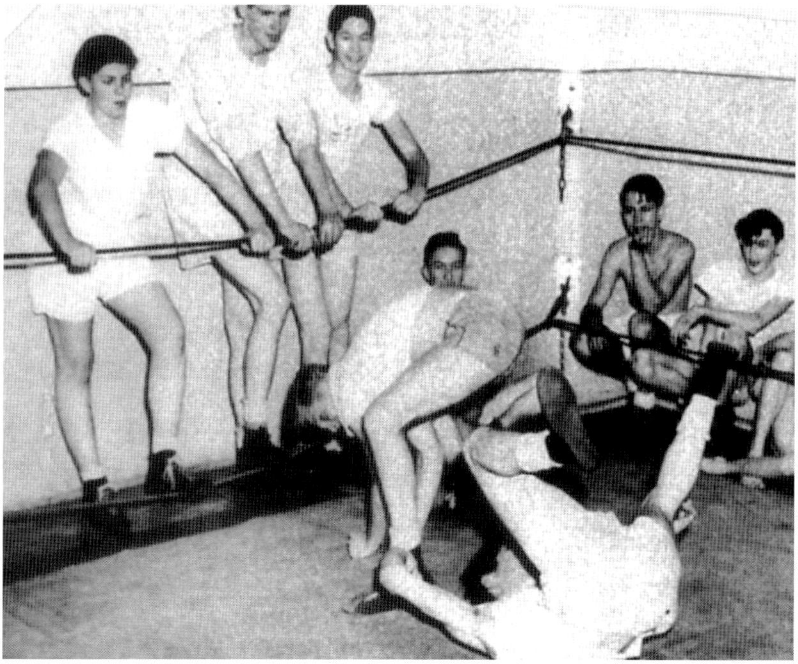

Boys will be boys. Pictured is physical education for less refined young men.

ACADEMICS

Shortly after the college became coeducational, in 1952, Father Murphy added to the curriculum. The new majors established were:

- art
- chemistry
- biology
- physics
- sociology
- business/economics (in 1953)

In 1953, the college established a program in medical technology. Students took three years at Villa. The fourth year was taken at one of the five area hospitals, including St. Elizabeth in Covington. After the successful completion of the fourth year, the students graduated from Villa.

In 1955, a similar program was established in Engineering—three years of study were taken at the college before the student moved on to one of four Engineering schools: the University of Dayton, the University of Kentucky, the University of Notre Dame or the University of Detroit. At the first three universities, after one year the student received his BA from Villa Madonna before returning to his university for the final year of Engineering. The University of Detroit had a three-year program where the student received his BA from Villa after two years.

The Psychology Department was established in 1962 by Father John Keller, while the Drama Department was created in 1972.

In 1976, Dr. Ronald Mann returned to the college to become academic dean, replacing Dean Jim Ebben. The following year, Dr. Mann established the Computer Science Department.

Then, in 1978, a full four-year degree program was set up in Nursing, again under the leadership of Dr. Mann. The major in Nursing actually went into effect in 1979 because of set-up restrictions. Today, it has become one of the largest departments.

EDUCATION

Bill Guilfoile was a 1952 graduate of the Education Department with a specialty in elementary education. As he was a longtime member of the department, one can only guess at the number of elementary teachers who were taught by Bill. He was also an accomplished musician, organist and vocalist.

They ought to be in pictures! Sister Lynette, SND, Sister Evelyn, SND, and Mr. William Guilfoile.

ENGLISH

Sister Agnes Margaret was one of the finest teachers the author has ever known. She was learned and inspirational, as beautiful on the inside as out. She tolerated no nonsense, as the author soon found out. She became one of his biggest supporters. She had a seventeenth-century wit without that age's morals or, rather, lack thereof. When the author's time comes, he wants to go to heaven where she is. She's keeping the angels in stitches.

Joseph Connelly was a popular mainstay in the English Department. He is seen at right with Sister

Above: Sister Agnes Margaret.

Right: An awesome threesome: Joseph Connelly, Sister Judith, OSB, and Sister Colleen, SND.

Sister Loretto Marie.

Judith, OSB, and Sister Colleen, SND. Joe was an oft-published poet. On the outside, he was a New York cynic; on the inside, he was a great romantic. Known to only a very few of his friends, every year on their anniversary he wrote his wife, Anita, a love poem. Sister Colleen is a good friend and classmate. She introduced the author to Willa Cather in English Seminar, senior year. *Oh, Pioneers*, *Death Comes for the Archbishop* and other classics by this Nebraskan writer are still in memory.

Sister Loretto Marie (seen above) was a librarian as well as an innovative English teacher. Her medieval literature class made meade minus the alcoholic content, and a model of Professor J.C. Adams's theory of the Globe Theater was built for her Elizabethan literature class.

Anglo-what?

"Thaes Cyninges Boceras" is Anglo-Saxon for "The King's Scribes,'" several of whom are pictured above, right. The writing on the board holds the key to Grendel's true identity.

LANGUAGES

Teacher turned missionary: Sister Emerita, CDP.

Sister Emerita, CDP, taught in the Modern Language Department for several years before leaving the college to do missionary work among the poor children of Madagascar. Political factions keep the children constantly in squalid conditions. An inspiring speaker, Sister spends most of her time in this country raising money for her mission. Every third year, Sister Emerita returns to Madagascar.

There were many scientists in Das German class. Larry Memering (below, first row, second from the right) appears to be giving close attention to Sister Rosina. In actuality, he was probably thinking of the date he had last week or his date for the weekend coming up. But he must have learned something about German; he graduated from Villa and became a three-two engineer at the University of Detroit.

Sprechen sie Deutsch?

Mathematics

Sister Elizabeth (second from right) was one of the college's first math teachers. She had a reputation for being able to teach math to many of us who were mathematically challenged.

Sister Julitta (seated next to her right) taught math as well as chemistry. The chairperson is Sister Rose (on the far left).

Fun with numbers?

History

A little to the left and a little to the right: Sister Mary Philip, SND, and Sister Mary Albert, SND.

Once again, two dedicated nuns who were in it for the long run, and what a great run it was for them, too—Sister Mary Philip, SND, and Sister Mary Albert, SND (left). One leaned a little to the left politically and the other a little to the right, and together they kept their department in the middle.

Dr. Raymond Hebert (right) was another outstanding addition to the faculty. He came from New England and stayed to become a "Kentuckian." Dr. Hebert has been, on occasion, chair of the History Department and academic dean, and he is currently head of the International Studies Program. He has led so many trips to Ireland that he thinks he's half Irish (actually, it is his better half, Maureen, who is Irish, but two shall become as one). The one thing that he refuses to give up about New England is his love for the Red Sox. Well, I guess that's okay—he spent a year in their minor league system.

The wise man from the East: Dr. Raymond Herbert.

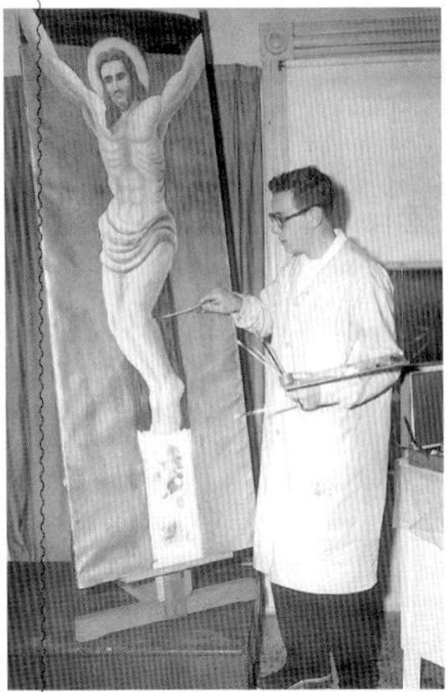

ART

On a religious retreat at Gethsemane (Kentucky), Don Smith (seen at left), who was without his glasses, thought that a small beam of light that enlarged behind a stained-glass window at Vesper service was a calling to the religious life. He was pleased to know that everyone else had the same vision.

Darrell Brothers was a longtime member of the Art Department. He was an outstanding teacher, devoting countless hours to his students and demanding their very best while always giving the best of his talent and experience to them and somehow finding time to produce a highly respected and well-known body of professional work. Darrell is seen at right with the members of his department: Darrell (left), Bernie Schmidt, Betty Drake and Ron Decker.

The Holy Family (seen opposite, top) was painted by Darrell Brothers in 1985 and donated to the college for its chapel in 1986. The following are some of the artist's comments about his work:

> *I was honored to paint this picture for the Thomas More chapel. It was suggested that Jesus might be shown as approximately the age of our students in order that they may more closely identify with him. As a result, this painting is different from traditional* Holy Family *pictures which show Jesus as a baby or sometimes a young boy; the chapel painting is similar to older paintings in other ways…Mary is enthroned and elevated in the painting, as in traditional paintings of this type, to emphasize her relationship to the College which was originally named Villa Madonna College.*

One of Darrell's protégés was Bernie Schmidt. Bernie was well known as a teacher and sculptor. He finished his academic career at Xavier University. Bernie's sculpture of Thomas More sits on the new campus.

Opposite, top left: Don Smith, one of our finest artists.

Opposite, right Members of the art faculty.

Left: The Holy Family.

Below: A statue of Thomas More by Bernie Shmidt, a Darrell protégé.

PHILOSOPHY

Seen at right are two longtime stalwarts of the Philosophy Department, Sister Camilla, CDP, and Dr. George Blair. They remained fast friends even after both of them had retired from the college.

Father Ramsey doesn't seem to get the joke in his ancient philosophy class (below). Some jokes apparently are not as funny as the ancient ones. But Father sure knew how to fill up a blackboard, sometimes bringing additional boards to augment his lectures. He also was famous for his "pinpoint bombing tests." Now that was something those World War II vets in his class understood for sure.

Above: Great minds/great friends.

Left: Maybe some jokes don't translate…

SOCIOLOGY

Mary Harmeling was quiet and unassuming, a true professional in every way. If there were a job to be done, it was "give it to Mary." And if it were possible, she accepted graciously.

In social work, Bob Berger was very highly regarded. He was also a joy to be around. He presided over the most popular table in the lunchroom, was the self-appointed spiritual advisor to the nuns and led discussions on the genius of Stephen Sondheim.

Two legends: Dr. Mary Harmeling and Professor Robert Berger (standing).

CHEMISTRY

Dr. James Swartz (seen in top photo below), formerly of the Chemistry Department, has established a long relationship with the college. He can measure his tenure by the length of his beard. He is now in the Computer Science Department.

Several members of the Chemistry Department are pictured in the bottom photo: Sister Rita Marie, chairperson (center); Dr. Ann Hicks (to Sister's right) and Dr. Jerry Franzen (far right). After Dr. Franzen retired from the college, he chose to teach chemistry at Newport Catholic High in order to better prepare students for college chemistry. Dr. Hicks, also retired, was a brilliant, unassuming member of the Chemistry Department. Her special talent was her ability to teach chemistry to nonscience persons, regardless of how long it took. She had infinite patience with those who tried.

Left, top: Dr. Swartz oversees a student experiment.

Left, bottom: More chemists.

Biology

The bio team: Dr. Bryant, Dr. Graham, Mr. Volker and Dr. Humphreys, longtime chairman of the department.

The Center for Ohio River Research & Education was established in 1998 as a private, nonprofit entity owned and operated by Thomas More College. The operation is based at the Field Station located on the Ohio River, twenty minutes away from campus. Working closely with federal, state and local authorities to monitor and improve water quality in the Ohio River is director of the program, Dr. Chris Lorentz.

At right, several of his students are collecting water samples. Fish are momentarily stunned to examine their condition before being returned to the water. In the background is a picture of the Field Station. In 1937, the year of the area's great flood, a marker at the very top of the building indicated that the river had reached a height of 75.1 feet.

On opposite page, bottom, a band of heavy hitters are at work. Across the table from Russ Steinhauer and Betty Johnson are Nick Frohlick, who became a player in the medical profession; future Kenton County judge William Schmaedecke; Jack Bruggeman, later Dr. Jack Bruggeman; and back across the table at the bottom of the picture is a man who became an eminent physician, Dr. George Kreyling, on staff of the University of Cincinnati.

Dr. Lorentz is instructing a student about an interesting-looking paddlefish.

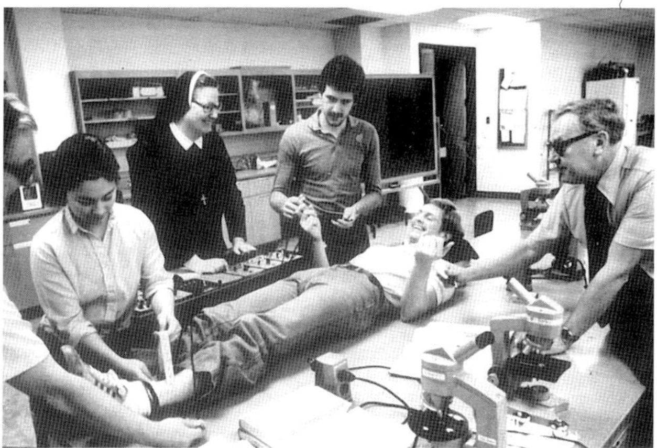

Dr. Humphreys and Sister Mary Laurence conduct an experiment in Dr. Frankenstein's lab.

Some serious lab work.

Physics

The professor and the atom.

Father John Schuler was a nationally known physicist. He was chosen as one of the scientists to observe the testing of the first atomic bomb. He is pictured at left with three of his outstanding majors, each of whom received grants to do doctoral work. They are (left to right): Richard Day (University of Maryland), Ronald Mann (University of Cincinnati) and Bonaventure Cahill (University of Cincinnati). These men went on to do significant work in their field. Dr. Mann did postgraduate work at the Max Pleunck Institute in Germany.

Dr. David Boyle has a hair-raising experience at right when student Ted Vogelpohl adjusts the control on the Van de Graaf generator to twenty thousand volts. Sophomore Rita Haneberg looks on approvingly.

A hair-raising experience.

Computer Science

Mr. Krebs of the Computer Department works on a state-of-the-art computer—well, for 1977.

Business/Economics

It appears that the boys just had a disconcerting look at their portfolios. From left to right are Mr. Richard Hoffman, Mr. Joseph Craycraft, Mr. Rudy Morrow, Mr. William McGrath and Mr. Tom Gilday Sr.

The Brain Trust.

Psychology

Pictured here are the current members of the Psychology Department. In rear: Dr. Kathie Langen and Dr. Larry Boehm; front: Dr. Maria McLean. Not shown is Dr. Bill Porter, now retired, a longtime staple in the department and an extremely popular person on campus.

Still going strong.

DRAMA

The Drama Department was established in 1972. Only one year later, it graduated its first major, Miss Peg Baker (at right). Peg was able to fulfill her requirements quickly thanks to the fact that the college had already been offering an associate degree in drama and only a few courses had to be added to the curriculum.

Dr. Kenneth Fitts (right, bottom) joined the Thomas More College faculty in 1970. Dr. Fitts was not only a fine teacher and play director, but he was also an excellent administrator. Dr. Fitts left the college in 1980 to produce and write soap operas, such as *The Guiding Light* and *As the World Turns*. He trained many writers and producers for the business and won an international reputation as a "soap" consultant.

Talk about doing it all. As a proud graduate of our former Drama Department (now called the Theatre Department), Professor Nelson has worked professionally as a director, an actor, a scene designer and a technician. Shown below, Mr. Nelson, the cowpoke on the left, plays a scene with the outstanding guest actor Adrian Sparks on the TMC stage in *Ned Durango Comes to Big Oak*.

We produced the emotionally tense *Anastasia* (opposite, top) at St. Aloysius School. Friday night was the opening night of the play. The gym/theatre was located above the cafeteria where, on Friday nights, bingo was held. (Back then, Friday nights meant fish and bingo for Catholics.) Throughout the production, we heard B-14, I-29, 0-70. But somehow the show must go on. It always does, you know. It's a tradition.

In the bottom photo, the newer additions to the department are shown. Alana Ghent (center) is the newest member of the Theatre Department. Next to her on her right is Mary Joe Nead, an addition to the communication area. Both ladies have performed splendidly, much to the pleasure of Professor Pat Raverty, chair (at right rear).

What one must do for one's art!

In with the new.

Opposite, top: The "Primus" graduate.

Opposite, middle: The man from the Ozarks.

Opposite, bottom: Across-the-board educated.

NURSING

The current nursing staff. *Left to right, seated*: Professor Denny, Professor Graham, Professor Cooper, Professor Cawhorn. *Standing*: Professor Owens, Dr. Torok (chairperson), Professor Tracy.

No Nurse Ratcheds here!

INTERNATIONAL PROGRAMS

"Mon Better Mon!"

Pictured here are the founders of the Jamaican project: Professor Tom Gilday with his son and daughter and two of their much-loved little friends.

Other international programs are also available. Dr. James Camp of the Sociology Department is the originator of the Mexican border project. Each summer, James and his volunteers go to Mexico to serve the people in whatever ways they are needed.

Dr. Ray Hebert (History) teaches a course on Ireland and has directed numerous visits there.

Dr. John Ferner (Biology) has led numerous adventures to some of the most exotic places in the world—Africa, Borneo, the Galapagos Islands and more. Kenya awaits.

Curricular Innovations

Dr. James Becker.

The Co-op Program was established by Sister Rita Marie (formerly Sister Casmira). It proved to be an immediate success, allowing participating students to gain meaningful work experience while earning some much-needed money.

Dr. Becker, formerly of the Psychology Department, succeeded Sister Rita Marie as director of Co-op, taking on the job full time because the program was growing in leaps and bounds. Upon his retirement, Dr. Becker opened a Christmas store in Florida, and thereafter, every day was Christmas for the Beckers.

TAP.

TAP (the **T**homas More College **A**ccelerated Degree **P**rogram) was launched by Dr. Dale Myers. Dr. Myers came to TMC from the University of Cincinnati, where he had extensive experience in nontraditional education. The program is an accelerated program designed for adults to achieve a degree in two years.

MUSIC

Sister Marcella was TMC's first music teacher. Here, she entertains her listeners playing the zither.

Although music has never been an academic major at the college, it has a long and honored tradition.

The faculty singers (seen opposite, top) were brought together for a Christmas concert with the chorus. We sang two songs, and we thought we were pretty darn good. But, by popular demand, we were never invited back. The names of the group will not be revealed in order to protect the perpetrators.

Matt Mattingly (below, right) is still playing his guitar for the patrons of his bed-and-breakfast in Maine. As a college student, he composed a song and played a portion of it in one of the early scenes of *Rain Man*. He is still receiving his residuals.

Seen opposite, middle, are TMC's version of the Andrews sisters plus one: (left to right) Mary Janet Hall, Joan Ossenbeck, Mary Ann Webster and Carolyn Stark.

Cacophony in B flat.

The lone guitarist.

In 1957, the school had its largest chorus to date. Mr. George Higdon (center) trained and directed its members.

Above, left and right: Yes, and then there's the singing, too.

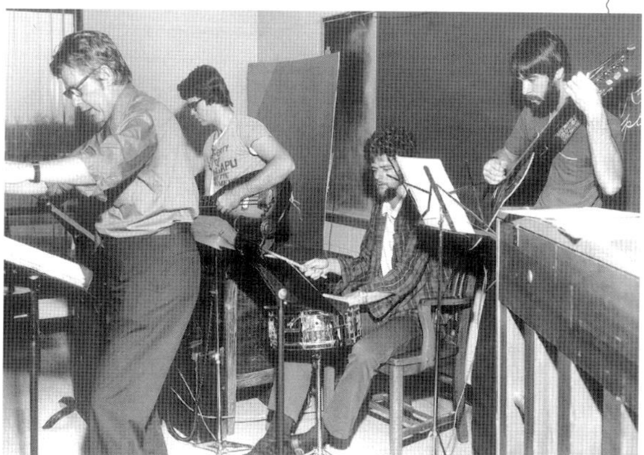

Right: Professor Robert Schaffer jams with three of his students. His son Mark, behind his father, is on the electric guitar, and son Gregg is on drums.

THE CAMPUS

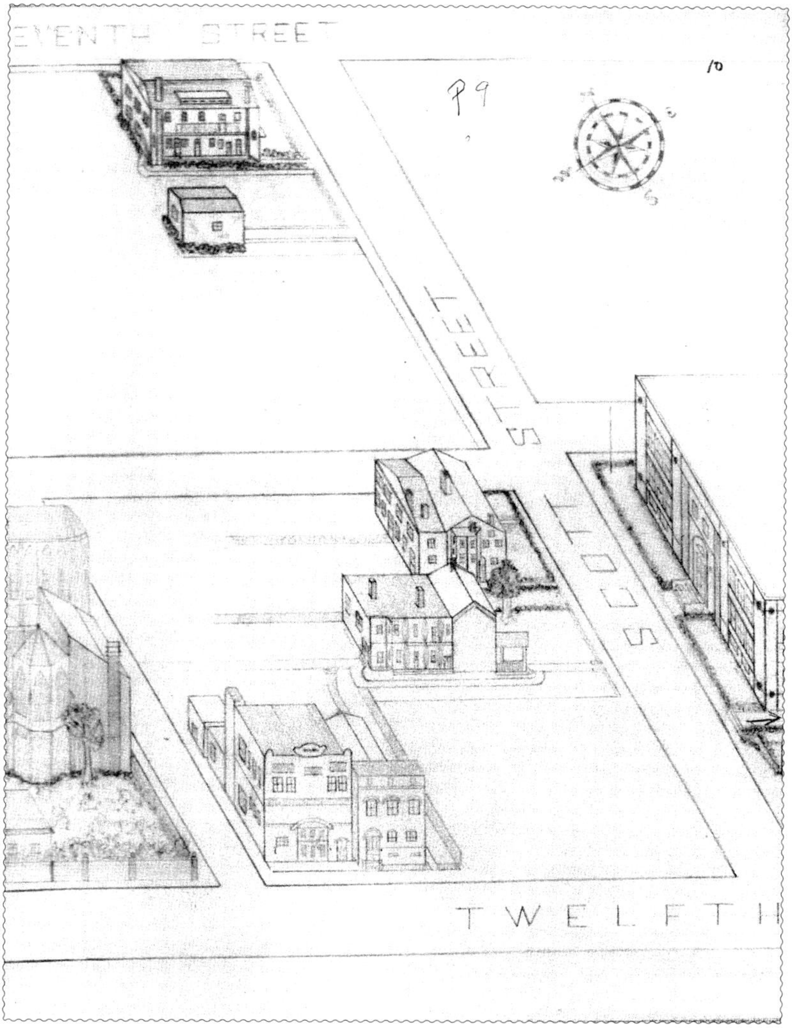

The heart of the old campus was at Twelfth and Scott Streets in downtown Covington.

EVOLUTION OF A BOOKSTORE

This closet-size room in the main building was the first bookstore. Class books were sold over the counter. Tuitions were paid here as well. Prior to 1952, the tuition was $42.50 a semester. Tuition then skyrocketed to $75.00 a semester.

Students crowded at the window to buy books at the first bookstore.

The current bookstore.

Our current bookstore is operated by Barnes & Noble and run by two bright and lovely young ladies, Elaine and Amanda (seen at right). The bookstore no longer collects tuition, and word has it that tuition is no longer $75.00—but we've saved the best phase for last.

The college acquired an old saloon on the corner of Twelfth and Scott Streets (below) in the summer of 1954. It reopened in the fall of that year as Talbot Hall (Talbot was the patron saint of alcoholics)—also known by the students as Alky-Hall. Your author was in class there shortly after classes began in the fall, when an old patron staggered in for an eye-opener, only to see a sweet little nun seated at a desk where the oaken bar had once stood. He quickly departed, and legend has it that the man swore off drinking forever.

The second bookstore.

Honoring the Namesake

With the original name of Villa Madonna, special attention was always given to Mary, the college's namesake.

The old statue of Mary has found a new home in Crestview Hills. Although May Crowning is no longer observed, many students and faculty stop to pray and give her homage.

Above: May crowning in the rose garden was always a special event.

Left: A new home for Mary.

Cabrini Hall

Juliets and their Romeos assemble outside of Cabrini Hall, next to the old firehouse on the left. The firehouse was acquired from the city in 1947. It became the home of biology, chemistry and math classes.

Cabrini Hall.

A College of Churches

The chapel.

The old campus was a college of churches, all within two blocks on Twelfth Street.

Mass was said daily in the college chapel (right).

The outside of St. Mary's Cathedral Basilica is modeled after Notre Dame de Paris in Paris, France. The north transept window, sixty-seven feet by twenty-four feet, is one of the largest stained-glass windows in the world. To the right of the main sanctuary is what is referred to as the Duveneck Chapel. Two murals and a triptych painting depicting three important events from the life of Christ are there. Frank Duveneck, a local artist of international fame, has his work on permanent exhibition in the Duveneck room of the Cincinnati Museum of Art.

The Monte Casino Chapel (opposite, left) is mentioned in *Ripley's Believe It or Not* as the smallest chapel in the world. It had been used by the Benedictine monks for prayer as they labored in the fields at some distance from their monastery in Covington.

Opposite page, right, Father Twaddell says daily Mass in the current college chapel, Crestview Hills. There is an architect's plan for a new chapel on campus, hopefully coming soon.

St. Mary's Cathedral.

The other churches were St. Joseph Church, one block to the east, and the Cathedral, one block to the west. Special feast days and events of a special nature—baccalaureates and graduations—were held at St. Mary's Basilica at Twelfth and Madison. The bishop's residence was at the Cathedral.

The old convent building that over the years had served so many different purposes was demolished. A new era begins. Crestview Hills, here we come!

Above, left: The Monte Casino Chapel as it stands now on campus.

Above, top right: The sacraments.

Above, bottom right: The end of an era.

CAFETERIA

Here is our intimate cafeteria as it was in 1957. Jay Rice (right) was a wonderful self-taught pianist who, after his retirement, played the nursing home circuit.

The intimate cafeteria.

PHYSICS DEPARTMENT

The Physics Department was at Mother of God's School on Sixth Street in downtown Covington. In Mother of God's auditorium on the third floor, two early Villa Players' plays were presented, *The Male Animal* by James Thurber and *Murder in the Cathedral* by T.S. Eliot. Choir robes, priests' vestments and priceless antique furniture were suddenly in short supply in convents and parishes throughout the area.

The Physics Department on Sixth Street.

The New Campus

Monsignor Murphy was a tough-minded businessman. He knew that the population was rapidly moving south in Kenton County. In 1954, he purchased 71.77 acres of the List property that fronted on Turkeyfoot Road. After tough negotiations with Bob and Alvin Gould, he was able to acquire another piece of property that ran to the present College Park Drive, but only after he purchased the first 9 acres adjacent to the List property for $9,000 an acre. The final purchase was the Krahmann farm, which lay behind the List farm. The total in 1971 was 223 acres. (From Monsignor Murphy's *Reflections.*)

The new building.

DEDICATION DAY, SEPTEMBER 28, 1968

Surprise! Surprise!

President Lyndon Johnson was on hand to dedicate the new campus. No one, not even Monsignor Murphy, knew for sure if he would come until a phone call made in flight by a Secret Service agent assured the monsignor of the president's arrival. It was a very proud day for the monsignor and a very proud day for the little college from Covington. "Though a campus we have not/Still we're the pride of 12th and Scott." What a day! A new campus and a new name—Thomas More College.

As part of the weeklong dedication ceremonies, the Villa Players presented Robert Bolt's famous play, *A Man for All Seasons*. Note the name of the players—the Villa Players. A bit of the old school came with us. It was an inspiring production by our students. Junior Mark Higdon played Thomas More.

Bob Jackson directed the dedication production. He is seen here in the new theatre space and on the set he designed for the production.

Dormitories

The first two dormitories were Marian Hall, the women's dorm, and Howard Hall, the men's dorm. They are the first two dormitories on the left in the photo below. A third dorm was added later, Ackerman Hall, on the right.

The dorms are spacious and well appointed, with two students to a room.

Murphy Hall was constructed in 1999, providing more dormitories. The building houses men and women in home-style suites for four.

The dormitories.

The rooms.

FACILITIES

The main floor of the library. Jim McKellog and his staff were of incalculable assistance to the author in completing this project.

The main buildings on campus are interconnecting. The Administration Building also houses Seiler Commons, which contains the dining hall and a utility space, eleven classrooms and originally a barbershop as well. Yep, a barbershop, long since out of business. The Academic Building contains classrooms and faculty offices. The Library Building not only contains the three floors of the library but also houses the theatre on the first and second floors.

"Fly Me to the Moon."

The Science Building was added in 1972, and all our students and faculty became one on the same campus. For the dedication of the science wing in 1972, the lunar rock was a big hit. None of our students was on the flight, so we had to borrow the rock from NASA.

Below, Coach Connor is at the podium humbly expressing his appreciation for the gymnasium being named after him. It was a proud day for a great local sports legend. Well done, Coach!

Coach Connor.

The Connor Convention Center, 1985.

The Five Seasons Country Club is a privately owned facility, but our students are allowed to use it at certain times of the day. It provides indoor swimming and tennis and… outdoor tennis and swimming!

Five Seasons Country Club.

Holbrook Center was completed in 1996. The center houses administration offices on the lower floor, and on the first level is a bookstore, snack bar, security offices, Steigerwald Hall (which is a multiuse space for meetings, banquets and the like). The center also contains a dance studio that doubles as a theatre rehearsal room.

A student center, at long last.

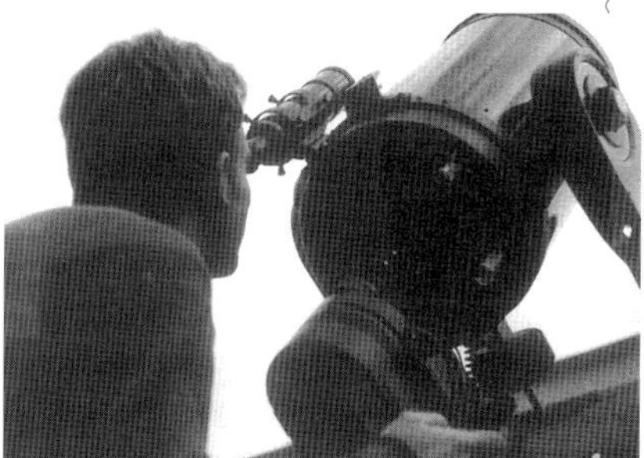

Recent grants have brought multiple other improvements to campus. Among them is the Eva G. Ferris Art Gallery, now situated in the front of the library. Other improvements to the library include additional classrooms, a new elevator system, multiple computer stations and a repositioned front desk for greater accessibility and security. New laboratories and new equipment for the science wing have also been provided.

Above, top: The New Bank of America Observatory—the sky's the limit!

Above, bottom: The facility has a retractable roof for better viewing, as this young stargazer is discovering. "One small step for man; one giant leap for mankind."

STUDENT ACTIVITIES

STUDENT NEWSPAPER

The literary staff of the *Triad* is hard at work putting together the school paper. A triad is, according to Webster's: "a group of three, esp. of three closely related or associated persons or things." The number three, of course, is a divine number, as in the Trinity.

Our school annual is called the *Triskele*. And what is a triskele, you ask? As the page at right tells us: "TRISKELE denotes a figure composed of three branches radiating from a center...The title has been selected because the symbol aptly signifies the distinctive characteristics of Villa Madonna College."

Above: "Read all about it!"

Right: The *Triskele*.

1956 Triskele

TRISKELE denotes a figure composed of three branches radiating from a center. The word is a variant of triskelion, a term of similar meaning, derived from the Greek. The title has been selected because the symbol aptly signifies the distinctive characteristics of Villa Madonna College:

the Unity

of its

Threefold Administrative Body--
The Reverend Provincial Superior of
The Sisters of Saint Benedict,
The Sisters of Notre Dame,
The Sisters of Divine Providence;

of its

Threefold Student Body--
Religious,
Young Women,
Young Men;

of its

Threefold Educational Culture--
Spiritual,
Intellectual,
Social.

VILLA MADONNA COLLEGE
COVINGTON, KENTUCKY

FRATERNITIES AND SORORITIES

What's a parade without a float?

Alpha Delta Gamma (ADG), in conjunction with the Hibernian Society, helped to sponsor the St. Patrick's Day parade in downtown Cincinnati. Pat Raverty of Rabbit Hash was one of the founders of ADG. He is still active in promoting the organization.

ADG generally entered a float in the St. Patrick's Day parade. The float seen at right was created for a Thomas More homecoming.

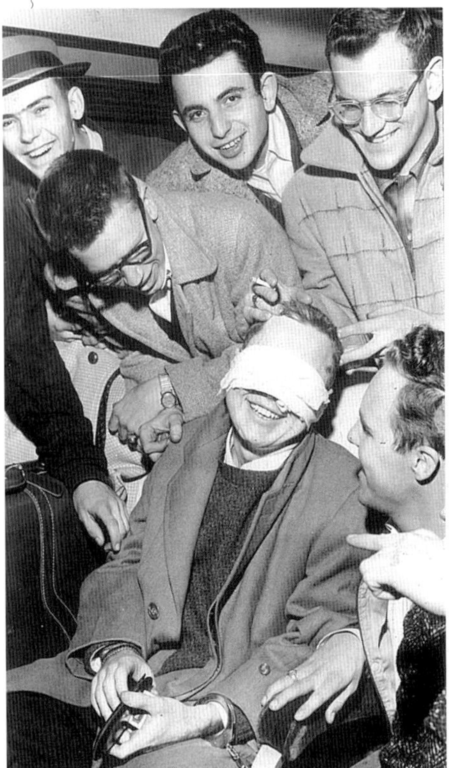

Sigma Alpha Lambda pledges captured and sent their pledge master, David Black, to Chicago as a joke. Blindfolded and handcuffed, he arrived in Chicago with insufficient funds for a return trip home. His ticket for the trip back to Covington was mailed to him three days later.

Opposite, top, Marilyn Remke serves punch to several of her sorority sisters. *Left to right*: Maureen Dailey, Nancy Gill and Maureen O'Malley.

Opposite, middle, The Gross brothers, Frank and Joe, are seemingly interested in learning about this punch thing. But they were more interested in the women

The blindfolding.

Refined and cultured to the max.

Designing brothers.

who later became their wives. Frank (alias Pee Wee) married Joan Muehlenkamp (left), and Joe married the punch server, Sandy Santel. But please note: the men did graduate despite the fact that Sister Julitta, their science teacher, wrote on each of their final exams, "Thank God, a knowledge of Science is not required for salvation." P.S. They were not science majors.

Dixie Chili Club

The Dixie Chili Club, TMC's very own Skull and Bones Society. It is so secret that the names of its members can never be divulged.

Shades of 'ol Eli.

PROMS AND OTHER DANCES

Proms are not the only big dances on campus. Fraternities, sororities and student government sponsor numerous dances throughout the year.

Many of our students become friends for life. This prom queen, Anne Marie Mielech, and her lovely attendant, Vicki Groh, certainly did.

Trying on his sister's crown, nothing! It was an obvious coup—inspired by the evil-hearted Lord Cottingham and the mysterious Lord High Sheriff of Nottingham.

Above: Lord Jim Lyon is telling his queen, Elaine Broering, "It's good to be the king."

Right: It was even better for Jim when he married the beautiful Monica McCoart (right). Tragically, they both died in the Beverly Hills Fire. RIP.

Fundraising

Seen below at left raising money for the new college is attorney Charles Deters, head of the campaign, and two of his fundraisers with the golden touch, alums James Fedders and Jack Kalker.

Below at right, Father Murphy helped register students for classes on the old campus.

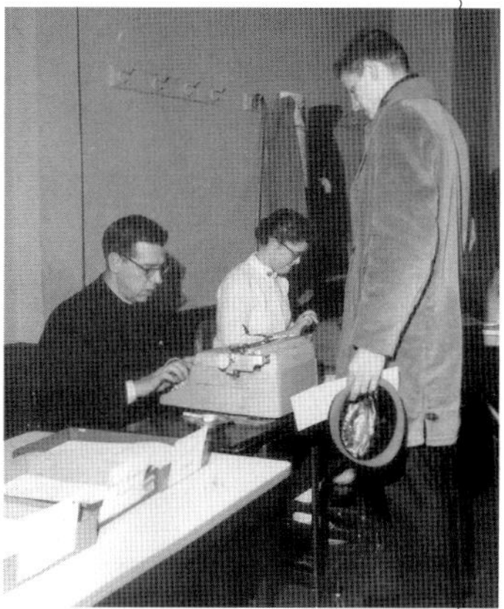

Above, left: Follow the money.

Above, right: Nothing else to do? When was the last time a college president helped out with registration? Maybe Father Murphy should have checked his job description.

John Bosco Society

The most beautiful faces of them all. These children enjoy Christmas with Santa, thanks to the wonderful work of the students of the John Bosco Society. The college motto: knowledge, leadership and service.

A priceless moment.

More Places and Faces... And Odds and Ends

Student President Jim Mann, "Mr. Everything," crowns Ann Honneman sweetheart queen at left, top. Jim was elected to so many positions that Father Murphy had to take note. When Jim was elected to yet another position, Father Murphy suggested that *he* was running the school, not Mr. Mann. Election denied.

Left, below, another queen and her court. The handsome young man in the rear is Larry Ries. He later became Lieutenant j.g. Larry Ries. He died in an aborted carrier landing, leaving behind a beautiful young wife, Nancy. Thank you, Larry, for your service to our country and to all like you—past, present and to come. Let freedom ring!

Opposite, middle, four of the six students are attending to business. Pat Deavy and George Deitmaring are more interested in playing to the camera.

Left, top: Mr. Everything.

Left, bottom: Keep 'em flying.

The hotties of 1956, and some of the nicest and most intelligent ladies on campus. Other hotties are in absentia. But you know who you are.

Some students were not quick enough to escape the long arm of the law. Police on motorcycles marked tires with rosin to enforce a one-hour parking limit. Students left class to move their cars on Scott Street or roll the markings up under the fenders. Classes continued uninterrupted.

And, speaking of Scott Street: we had an anonymous, unauthorized Alma Mater that went in part: "By the Licking River muddy/ Stands our school so small and cruddy… Though a campus we have not/Still we're the pride of Twelfth and Scott."

Above, right: Two out of six isn't bad.

Left: The law picture.

THE SAGA OF THE PORTRAIT AND THE BUST—A MYSTERY

Case number one. The famous portrait of Thomas More suddenly vanished from its wall space. Even Columbo was stumped. Then a message left in the night made a demand: Sister Mary Philip was to deliver several hundred dollars to the Glenn Rendezvous Hotel and gambling emporium (a well-known mob hangout) at midnight of the following day. She was to give the money to a tall doorman known as "The Dwarf." No one knows if Sister actually went that night. But the portrait just as mysteriously reappeared at graduation. No one ever discovered the identity of the culprits, although Dean "turned detective" Hoppenjans had his suspicions.

Case number two: even more bizarre. The bust of Thomas More disappeared from its honored place in the library. Only this time, the bust literally took flight to various places across the country, sending back postcards and snapshots to document his travels. One was a snapshot from a sunny beach in Florida, where the divine Thomas was seen sunbathing in a nifty pair of Foster Grants.

Another was of a visit to Wrigley field for a game. But that year, the bust returned by helicopter during our outdoor graduation. This time, "Detective" Hoppy devised a foolproof plan. He reasoned the culprits were probably seniors by now, so he let them graduate. The plan worked brilliantly. And no further incidents have occurred.

ATHLETICS

GOLF

Fore!

The 1956 men's golf team was perhaps our finest. Bob Schultz (center rear) was one of the best golfers in the area. But they all could play. Father Welp of the English Department was their coach. He could play a little bit, too.

For the record, the men's tennis team in the late '80s was another outstanding team.

VOLLEYBALL

Krissy and Kimi Flynn, twins (second and third from left, first row), were two of the finest athletes in school history. In addition to volleyball, they also starred in basketball and softball. They are justifiably in the Thomas More Sports Hall of Fame.

Double your pleasure.

Basketball

Left, top: our first basketball team, 1946. Number 13 in the front row is Don Hellman, who will become captain of the '47 team. Today he is better known as Monsignor Hellman.

If you have a basketball team, you have to have cheerleaders. It's a beautiful tradition.

Sports were in hiatus at the college during the Korean War (1950–53). Basketball resumed in 1954, and baseball a year later.

Pictured at right is the 1954 basketball team, a fine group of athletes. Several of them have gone down as among the finest athletes to play at Thomas More–Villa Madonna. Number 22 is Larry Staverman. And who is Larry Staverman?

After an outstanding career at Thomas More, this Newport Catholic grad was drafted

Above, left top: God was on our side. First basketball team, 1946.

Above, left middle: Yea, team!

Above, right: Some of our finest—1954 team.

Left: Larry Staverman (#21) for the Cincinnati Royals.

by the Cincinnati Royals. Larry is #21 for the Royals. Note the names of two of his teammates, #14, Oscar Robertson, and #31, Jack Twyman.

After playing a season with the Royals and a season with Detroit, Staverman decided to call it quits in the NBA. He spent two seasons as an assistant coach at Notre Dame under Johnny Dee. In 1967, he became the first coach of the Indiana Pacers of the American Basketball Association, compiling a two-year record of 40-47. He also coached with the New York Nicks in 1977–78, posting an 18-21 record.

After his retirement from basketball, Larry was active in the NFL. He served as general manager for the Cleveland Municipal Stadium until it was demolished in 1996 and then took a position as a consultant with the Nashville County Metro government, where he helped to oversee the construction of the Tennessee Titans' stadium, which opened as Adelphi Stadium in 1999.

Two more future picks to the Royals.

Larry returned home to northern Kentucky and remained involved in various types of volunteer work. He died unexpectedly in July 2007. His former high school and college teammate Jim Weyer said of him, "We were really close—in each other's weddings and all that. He was a wonderful man." You said it, Jim. He was a role model on and off the court. And by the way, Larry had a wonderful education—sports star and physics major plus all of the above.

At right, number 32, Gerry Thelen (up left), was a stellar big man for the Rebels, as we were named then. Gerry was drafted by the Royals and was the last man cut that season. Number 52, Dan Tieman (center), would later play a year with the Royals.

Brian O'Conner (left) went from Covington Latin (a small prep school) to Thomas More and, at age twenty, on to the New York Knicks.

And the basketball team wasn't afraid to mix it up with the big boys, either. They played mighty Xavier a variety of games and won two: 85–64 in 1969–70 and 65–64 in 1972–73. They also lost a heartbreaker to Xavier, 72–70, in 1976–77.

The battle of the big men. TMC's Brian O'Conner and Todd Kofler battle Xavier's #44 Joe Sunderman; ready to spring into action for TMC is Ronny Dawn.

We took on some of the biggest powers in the Northeast. When the author was attending graduate school in New Haven, Connecticut, the only person he met who had heard of Villa Madonna was a basketball fan from Villanova.

Opposite, top, fans are seen returning from our game against Niagara University in 1959–60. The team and

Above, left top: Think big—Brian O'Conner.

Above, left middle: From the land of the giants.

Left: Here we are battling mighty Holy Cross. Ron Albrink and Dan Tieman defend.

Fans at the Niagara University game.

fans had reason to be proud and happy. VMC 77, Niagara 73. Go Rebs! So send in the cheerleaders!

Below left was the gym in St. Benedict's grade school. Moon backboards, little out of bounds space, a locker room with no lockers, benches for your clothing and two cold showers. But here's the rub: not only were the intramural games played here on Sunday afternoons, but the varsity also practiced here on the other days of the week until the new on-campus gym was built in 1989. As a concession to modernity, new backboards were eventually installed. And this is where the teams that beat the likes of Xavier and Niagara practiced.

No place like home.

BASEBALL

Below, left, first baseman Tom Ginney goes airborne for a throw. Tom was one of the Ginneys to matriculate at Villa–Thomas More. In his *Personal Reflections*, Monsignor Murphy wrote, "Among the many great families [that welcomed me] was that of Tom and Bessie Ginney, whose home was always full of people and music, food and good times. The two oldest children, Margee and Tom, were students at Villa and the younger, Roseanne and Jimmy, were still in St. James grade school (Ludlow). I cannot say enough about the family." And, oh yes, the hitter in the insert below right is monsignor-in-waiting Don Hellmann. He excelled in baseball, too.

Coach Weyer was also a fine baseball player. At right he is seen in the happy days of the early 1970s. By the mid-'70s, his team had fallen upon hard times, so much so that Weyer sometimes had to play right field until a player could get out of class to replace him. As always, studies came first. But too bad Weyer had to come out. He was probably the best player on the team. On the other hand, Weyer's 1971 team posted an outstanding 16-7 season, including 4 wins over Northern Kentucky and a win over Xavier. Once again—Go Rebs!

Top: From the court to the diamond: Coach Weyer.

Middle and bottom: The Ginneys.

Of course, our finest baseball player was David Justice. He has two World Series rings, was a three time all-star and Rookie of the Year in 1990. There is little doubt that the sweet swinger from little Thomas More will one day be in the Major League Hall of Fame. If you look closely at his rookie baseball card at left, you will see that it has been personally autographed. And, most importantly, David is a good guy who never forgets his friends.

Thomas More's first baseball field was built by Coach Connor and his players. It was located across Thomas More Parkway from where the Five Seasons Country Club is located.

Our new field is built on the front of the property along Turkeyfoot Road. The field has become a very handsome playing space today. But there were more than a few problems at the outset. When the coach returned with the team from their spring training camp at St. Bernard College in Alabama, the administrator who was put in charge of overseeing the project proudly announced that the field was in readiness for the opener just a few days away. Coach Connor looked around and nodded. "Are we going to have a backstop?" Sure enough, no backstop. With coach back on the job, the problem was solved by opening day. The picture at left, shows a workman installing the object in question. But that isn't the whole story. The administrator announced that an underground sprinkling system had been installed. Terrific, right? Wrong. The field hadn't been turtle-backed for drainage, so the water just pooled on the surface. He had essentially put a sprinkling system in a swamp.

Top: Cooperstown, here comes David Justice!

Middle: "If you build it they will come."

Bottom: Well, you can't think of everything, I guess.

It seemed like a good idea at the time.

CROSS COUNTRY

When Thomas More needed another sport to remain eligible for NAIA Championship play, Father Holtz (above in sweater) of the Psychology Department helped basketball coach Jim Weyer start a cross country team—"of sorts." The team was to consist of the men's basketball team with the added benefit of conditioning the players for basketball. As it turns out, different sports require different conditioning. Result: it almost killed the players. At one meet, the team had to cross McMicken Avenue, a busy street on the UC campus. By the time our guys got to the traffic light, the crossing guard had gone home, and the team had to wait for the light to change before they could finish the race. Today, we have a real cross country team.

FOOTBALL

Our first football team huddles up.

The new Bank of Kentucky field.

In 1991, football came to Thomas More. Our first game was played at Dixie Heights High School in Erlanger against Kentucky Wesleyan. We won! The biggest college football game in town used to be the University of Cincinnati versus Xavier. But after Xavier dropped football, who could have imagined that the biggest college game in town would become Mount St. Joseph versus Thomas More?

The Teams of Thomas More Today

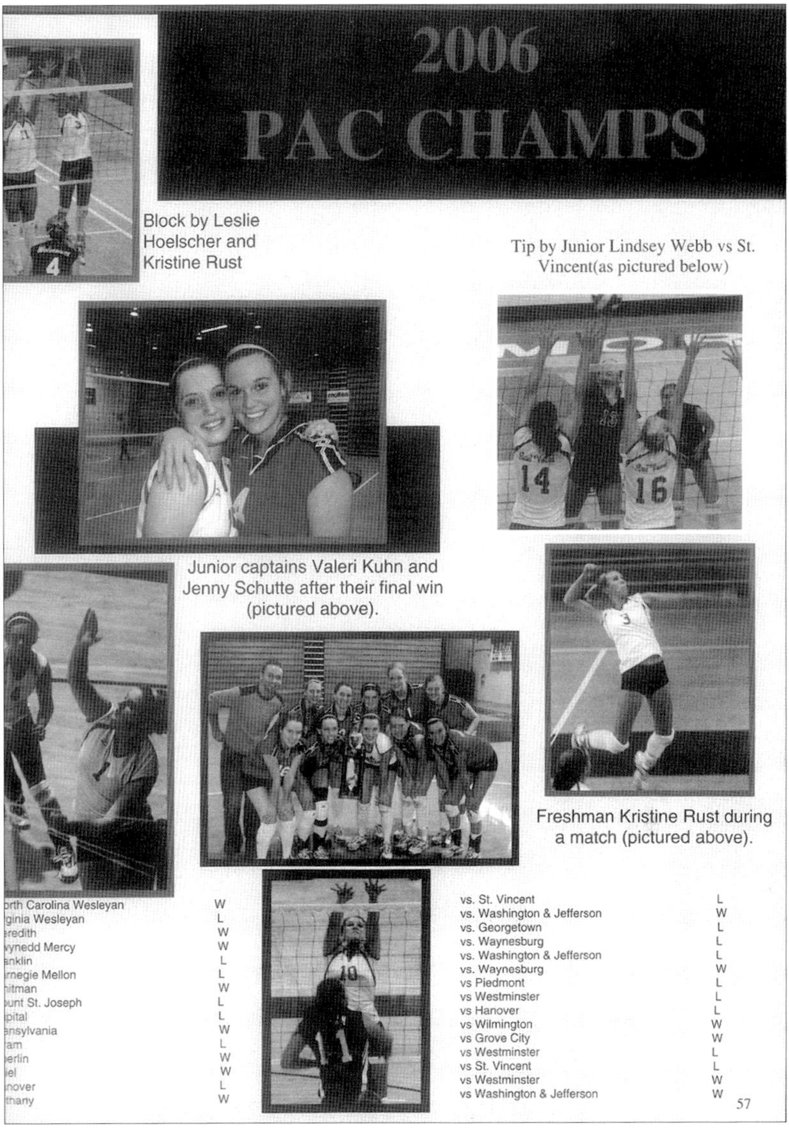

Women's volleyball.

Men's Tennis
Justin Egan
David Sheeley
Joe Ruzick
Johnny Bergman
Mark Lucas
Michael Selm
Terence Toone
Coach
Matt Finke
Men's Team
Bergman, Justin Egan, Ben Graham, Mark Lucas, John
Joe Ruzick, Michael Selm, David Sheeley , Ryan
Thompson, Terence Toone
59

Women's Tennis

Alma Murga

Emily Prescott

Haley O'Connell

Katie Trauth

Monica Pharo

Whitney Reis

Senior Whitney Reis (pictued above)

Alma Murga (pictured above)

Haley O'Connell (pictured above)

Coaches
Jenny Fette
Claire Krumme

Women's Team
Alma Murga, Haley O'Connell, Monica Pharo, Emily Prescott, Whitney Reis, Katie Trauth

58

Men's Basketball

Congrats Seniors!
Ed " Cleve " Thornton # 24
Mike Selm # 10

MC taking the ball out against Grove City. Display showing off seniors
rnton and Mike Selm. Pictured middle is Mike Selm and the rest of the
esburg. Top right, Junior Joe Langley boxing out and Junior Jeremy Abell
three point range.

TMC Women's
2007 Presidents' Athletic

Top Left: Seniors Megan Wood, Brooke Warner and Amber Sims after winning the PAC
Championship vs. Westminster at home. Below, Coach Brian Neal cutting down the rest of the ne
Kristen Humphrey and Megan Wood listen intently to Coach Neal during halftime. Pictured midd
The Connor Crazy Fan section, below the 2007 TMC team after the big win over Westminster.
Pictured bottom middle, Junior Jenna Kelsch vs Wittenburg. Pictured top right- Junior Kristen
Humphrey taking a breather while Sophomore Brandi Mahar and Junior Jennifer Teski attack on
offense. Bottom Right- Sophomore Alex Gee drives past Calvin in the NCAA Tournament Round

Thomas More
PAC Cinfield
(pictured top left)
Softball PAC Champions
(pictured top middle)
Kaycee Bischoff
(pictured left)
Jamie Wisenall
(pictured right)
(below left to right) Stacy Barry, Jennifer Lang, Kim Kreimer, Laura McDonald

Softball.

Baseball

Brad Ketterer
(pictured left)

Brad McIntoash
(pictured below)

Fred Riess
(pictured right)

Jake Brown
(pictured left)

Kyle Wewe
(pictured below left)

Matt Klausing
(pictured above right)

Joe Berling
(pictured right)

Johnny Lee
(pictured left)

Chris Fishburn
(pictured left)

Golf

Coaches
Marc Barone, Bob Schultz, Al Wright

Team
Marty Arnzen, Jon Aydt, Chris Bosse, John Donlan, Tim Hall, Tyler Heidel, Joe Ruzick, Scott Weeks

all

Weeks

Jon Aydt

Marty Arnzen

Coach
Mark Hannahan

Team
Ali Denton, Kera Fletcher, Molly Jendzio, Tyneesha Lamendola, Carolyn Lampman, Teri Morris, Alicia Paff, Katie Raverty, Brooke Warner, Theresa Weichold

69

Ben Bach
(pictured above)

Coach
Michael Reed

Team
Kila Hanrahan
Ben Bach
Larry Stange
Justin Egan
Chad Schmidt

Kila Hanrahan
(pictured above)

Cross Country

09/09/2006
Wittenberg Invitational
Springfield, OH

09/15/2006
NKU Norse Classic
A.J. Jolly Park

09/30/2006
Earlham CC Invitational
Richmond, IN

10/13/2006
Wilmington Invitational
Wilmington, OH

10/21/2006
Southeastern Classic CC Meet
Berea, KY

10/27/2006
PAC Championships
Waynesburg, PA

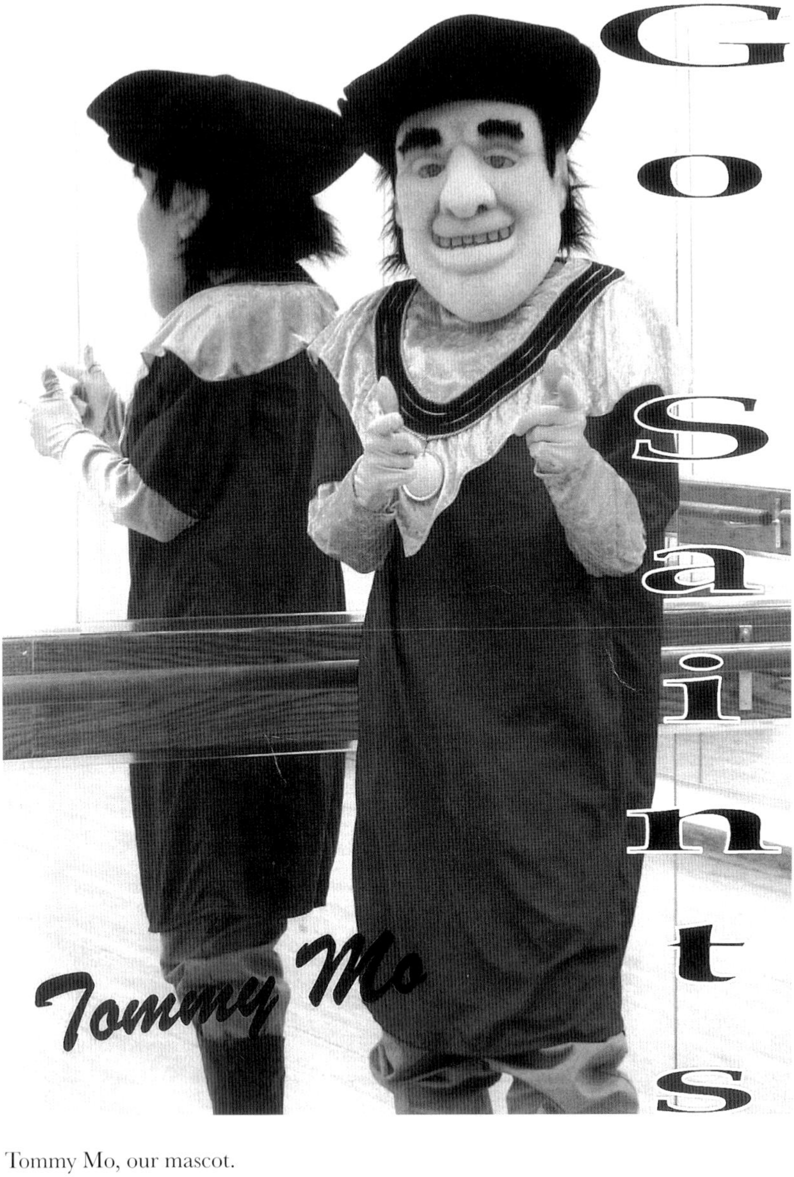

Tommy Mo, our mascot.

SPECIAL EVENTS

Academic Events: Conferences and Lectures

Seiler Commons was jammed with people from all over the area in 1972 for our Futuristic Conference to hear the likes of Buckminster Fuller of geodesic fame, poet Allen Ginsberg and other notables.

The Great Balloon Race

The Great Balloon Race launched from campus in 1977. There were lots of thrills, fun and games for the kids and plenty to eat for everyone.

STUDENT FASHION SHOW OF 1977–78

Here's a fashion show for the ladies. The lovely Marilyn Kroger models a beautiful wedding gown. The ladies loved the event, but it made the guys on campus very nervous.

Left: The student fashion show of 1977–78. Looking good. And the winner is—Terry Jefferson. Not even close, man.

Right: Uh-oh, guys.

A truly special gift from Monsignor Hillenmeyer.

THOMAS MORE BIRTHDAY CELEBRATION, 1978

At left, seated next to Dr. Hebert, who hosted the event, are (left to right) Dr. Richard Marius, an editor of the *Complete Works of Thomas More*, and Dr. J.H. Hester, of Yale University, who delivered the principal address.

Left, below, Monsignor Hillenmeyer chats with Cardinal Bernadin as Bishop Ackerman and TMC president Richard Degraff look on. Monsignor Hillenmeyer established the Hillenmeyer lecture series in honor of his family. It brings some of the finest theologians and religious thinkers to campus. The event culminates Thomas More Week, which celebrates our patron.

NOTABLE FACULTY AND ALUMS

Gone rogue.

The answer to a trivia question.

An old acquaintance won't be forgotten.

Mr. Harry Beck, left, according to Monsignor Murphy's writings, was, like many of us young pups, something of a rogue elephant. Now there's a mixed metaphor for you. Sorry, Sister Agnes Margaret, I'll do my penance later. Anyway, after a talk with Murphy, ol' Harry straightened up fast. He became the excellent student he was always capable of being, a fine administrator at the college and, later, the founder of Beckfield College.

Michael Burch created the Academic Tax team that won national attention and earned high-quality scholarships for many tax team members. But here's something you didn't know. Mike is the answer to a trivia question. Who did the Reds release from their farm system to make room for Johnny Bench? That's right, another catcher—Mike Burch. At left (middle) he is seen with his wife, Carol, in front of Holy Spirit School in Covington, where the couple enjoyed their wedding reception years before, when it was known as St. John's.

Left, bottom, Maryline Glover, a beloved member of the Sociology Department, advises a student in 1982. Unfortunately, she was stricken with a heart attack in the classroom and had to be rushed to the hospital, but she was DOA. The hardest thing about writing

this book is realizing how many of our dear friends are no longer with us.

Dr. Willet, pictured at left with his wife, Dorothy, was an outstanding teacher and a fine practitioner of his science. The J.E. Willet Treatment Center was dedicated in his name. The center is located on Burlington Pike in Florence. Dr. Willet and his wife are active members of Mother of God parish in Covington.

Ms. Mary Schwab (left middle) was a secretary and an assistant registrar. The Mary Schwab Outstanding Staff Member of the Year Award was named after her.

Fittingly, Mary Dorough (left, bottom) was the first recipient of the Mary Schwab award. She was a longtime secretary who for a great while served Monsignor Murphy as his personal secretary. Later, she chose to reenter the secretarial pool after monsignor left the college. She was always willing to type a letter for a friend in a rush. Thanks, Mary, for helping so many of us out in a pinch.

Jeanne Pike (opposite, top) was seemingly put in charge of the Audio Visual Department soon after God created the world. Jeanne almost defies description. She was always there in her office ready to assist you with your AV needs and to offer you the strongest

Left, top: Dr. Joseph Willet.

Left, middle: A name to remember.

Left, bottom: Another outstanding secretary.

cup of coffee you've ever tasted. In her younger days, she smoked a pipe and little cigars and tried not to let it be known that she was concert trained on the English horn. After all, she did have an image to uphold. She loved basketball, but she liked even more playing gin rummy at half time with her buddy, Sister Mary Laurence. After she retired, she took art lessons at the college and has become quite good at her landscape paintings.

Physics, Math and Astronomy have become closely linked. *Below, left to right, standing*: Dr. Lameier, Father Enzweiler, Dr. Christenson, Dr. Wells, Dr. Riehemann. *Seated*: Professor Taylor, Mary Ann Heimert and Dr. Ryle.

Above, right: Jeanne Pike: one of a kind.

Above: A special simpatico—physics, math and astronomy.

Clockwise from top left: Secretary to the academic deans forever: Mrs. Joy Nolan, a real sweetheart; plant engineer Dave Neyer; sports kept in proper perspective; the kitchen staff's representative, Beth Kluemper, several times Employee of the Month.

Above: Security.

Opposite, bottom, Tommy More is the dog and Rob Marshall is his driver. You have to look carefully to see Tommy. There is more to him than his black nose. But his favorite thing to do is ride in the golf cart. Then it's time for a nap. Vandals beware.

Dave Neyer (opposite, top right) helps run the family winery, Atwood Hill, in Morningview, Kentucky. Or, as we like to say in Kentucky, "It's just a spit down I-75." And believe us, it's well worth the trip.

Opposite, middle right, Coach Terry Connor, the athletic director, represents the whole department. And if there's any man who can do it, it's Coach Connor.

Below, Sandra Cuni brought recognition to Thomas More through the publication of her poetry. She died unexpectedly in 1973. Sandra was also a wonderful teacher of writing. Today, the Cuni Award is given via a schoolwide competition to the outstanding student writer of the year.

VMC/TMC is a college of fine scholars and artists, some of whom we have already mentioned, such as Jim Nelson. So let's mention but a few more.

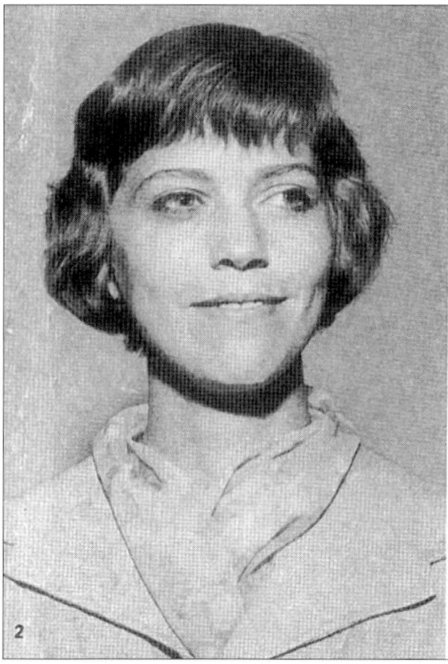

Full of life now, compact,
visible,
I, forty years old the eighty-
third year of the States,
To one a century hence or any
number of centuries hence,
To you yet unborn these, seeking
you.

When you read these I that was
visible am become invisible,
Now it is you, compact, visible,
realizing my poems, seeking me
Fancying how happy you were if
I could be with you and
become your comrade;
Be it as if I were with you.
(Be not too certain but I
am now with you.)

Walt Whitman

A prestigious award is given in honor of Sandra Cuni.

ON THE SCHOLARLY SIDE...

Cheer for Old Notre Dame.

Who is who?

Dr. Paul Tenkotte.

After winning a scholarship to Notre Dame Law School, Larry Wichmann received congratulations from Father Deye (left). Father Deye himself received his graduate degree in history from Notre Dame. Father Dye was nationally known for his involvement in the civil rights movement.

Who's who in American universities and colleges, vintage 1958: Left, middle: *front row, left to right*: Judy Higdon, Juanita Ziegler, Pat Richard, Madonna Jack; *back row*: Herb Luken, George Thelen and Paul Simon. George and his brother Gerry, not pictured here, have been longtime supporters of the college, both financially and with their commitments of their time and talents.

Paul Tenkotte (left bottom) has recently produced his extensive *History of Northern Kentucky*, coauthored with James Claypool of Northern Kentucky University. Dr. Tenkotte is seen here among the memorabilia he brought together for his display on Abraham Lincoln at the Behringer-Crawford Museum in Devoe Park.

Dr. Bryant (opposite, top) has lectured and written extensively on the flora of Kentucky. Without a doubt, he is the foremost authority on Kentucky plant life. Put him on the artistic side of the ledger as well. He has also published poems and short stories about his beloved home state.

Dr. William Bryant.

Dr. Ronald Mann.

Dr. Mann (above, right) wrote an important textbook for the field of physics, *The Classical Dynamics of Particles, Galilean and Lorentz Relativity*. Dr. Mann did postgraduate work at the Max Pleunck Institute in Germany.

Dr. Lynch-Knoll (right, top) has published a new book in communication, entitled *Communication Skill Book: Practice to Theory.* It is published by the Kendall Publishing Co.

Father Ketteler (right, bottom) has written many articles and books in addition to his position papers for the Diocesan Bishops of Kentucky. His writings have become internationally known, with more recent website hits from India and Latin America.

Right, top: Dr. Patricia Lynch-Knoll.

Right, bottom: Father Ronald Ketteler.

ON THE ARTISTIC SIDE...

Appalachian roots.

Two very good friends; two very different paths.

Dr. Sherry Stanforth is the chair of the Creative Writing Program. She is a noted poet and song writer who performs with Sunset Dawn, her small musical group of four women performing on strings and woodwinds. All of Sherry's writings and songs are about her roots, the Appalachian Mountains of Kentucky.

Talking about the arts, here's an often-asked question: what can you do with a theatre degree? Answer: many things, both in and out of the profession.

At left, Mardia Bishop and Keith Brush star in *A Far Country*, a play about the experiments of the young Sigmund Freud. Mardia was a brilliant double major in history and drama. When she was finishing her doctorate in history of theatre at Ohio State, the chairman of the department contacted the author to see if we had any more students like her. He was willing to give them a scholarship out of hand. Today, she is busy raising her family, teaching part time and managing to write books on an interesting topic. The titles speak for themselves: *Popporn: Pornography in American Culture* and *Mommy Angst: Motherhood in American Popular Culture*. As you might guess, these are not pro-porn books. Keith Brush is a very fine actor who has made at least one appearance locally at the Ensemble Theatre. He is currently living and acting in Los Angeles.

Opposite, top left, Buz Davis (right) plays Reverend Chasuable in one of his earliest roles at Thomas More. Buz's résumé is too long to go into much detail. In addition to his acting credits, he has directed and worked

Above: *The Importance of Being Earnest.*

Right: A similar start, a different finish: Tom Scott and Jackie Fink.

as a production stage manager. Mr. Davis performed readings with various orchestras, including the Boston Symphony and the Esplanade Orchestra. Mr. Jim Gilliece (behind sofa), known as "Jimmy," came to Thomas More as PR director. He stayed on to become a drama major. For several years after graduation, he toured nationally as a stand-up comedian. Jim and his wife, Patty, now own and run Chez Nora's restaurant in the Mainstrasse. Customers have said they have the best pork chops in America. The author has tried them, and he wouldn't disagree. Sue Banks (standing up left) also lived for a time in New York, where she started her own theatre company and also directed. Today, Sue is the manager of the Kenton County Library, Erlanger branch, where she continues to present live entertainment of various kinds for both young and old.

Tom Scott was a very successful writer for numerous off-off-Broadway revues. He was certainly one of the finest playwrights to come out of TMC. Today, Tom lives in Florida, where he buys and raises show horses for national and international Dressage competitions. Jackie Fink was an extremely talented actress with a natural propensity for playing styles of performance. She received her MFA from Case Western Reserve, and after a successful professional career, she entered the business world. Today, she is the regional manager for American Nursing Care, overseeing a $60 million business.

Above, left: Leave it to a grad!

Above, right: A little lady with great drive and great talent.

A former drama student, Nancy Klayer, started the Thomas More summer theatre. The program was to bring drama graduates back to campus to do plays with current students. Nothing helps to expand the talent level like performing with and observing the more experienced. The program still continues on a periodic basis. That's Nancy, in the photo above, left: middle row, second from the right. The production was *Charlie's Aunt*.

And last, but far from least, is Lynn Meyers (above, right). Lynn is the producing-artistic director of the Ensemble Theatre of Cincinnati. Again, Lynn's résumé is too long to give in much detail. She has directed numerous shows at the Ensemble Theatre, including her own, *Package Deal*. She also directed her original musical, *Starstruck*, in Canada. Her casting credits include work for MTM, CBS, PBS, BBC, HBO Paramount and, her favorite, serving as location casting director for Castle Rock's *Shawshank Redemption*. She is also the recipient of the 2000 YMCA Career Woman of the Year Achievement Award, and more recently, she received a 2008 Woman of Over-the-Rhine Award.

So with an across-the-board education in theatre and a strong liberal arts background, it seems as if you can do just about anything!

And Two Fond Farewells

Professor Nancy Bruns.

Professor Nancy Bruns began her career at Thomas More in the History Department, and a fine teacher of history she was. But a critical need developed in the registrar's office, so Nancy took on the job of head registrar. For the rest of her career, she ran an incredibly efficient office while managing to earn a master's degree in theology. She was one of the first to offer a course in women's studies. That warm smile that you see captures the essence of this wonderful woman.

Dr. Bob Jackson.

Dr. Jackson, who received his doctorate after leaving Thomas More and starting his own independent film company, had always been a strong advocate of a major in drama. Happily, he saw his dream come to fruition even though he was not a part of it. But Bob left an enormous legacy for others to build on. Fittingly, his last appearance on the TMC stage was in the role of Prospero in Shakespeare's *The Tempest.* Before leaving his island, Prospero bids farewell to his faithful servant, Ariel: "And like the great globe itself, yea, all which it inherit, shall dissolve and like this insubstantial pageant faded, leave not a rack behind. We are such stuff as dreams are made on, and our little life is rounded with a sleep." Sleep well, my friend. Sleep well.

CONCLUSION

And now, in a way, back to how it all began.

Two nuns of the Order of St. Benedict stand behind the altar in the infirmary at their Mother House on Amsterdam Pike in Villa Hills. On the left is Sister Carmella, 101 years old, and her natural sister, Sister Samuel, 98. Both are spry and sharp and always ready to go. Sister Carmella was in one of the first college courses given on the grounds, which is now the site of Villa Madonna High School.

And what's it all about? Graduation!

ABOUT THE AUTHOR

Dr. Mielech is a professor emeritus at Thomas More College, where he is also an alumnus (class of '54). During his thirty-three years teaching at the college, he served as the chair for the Department of English and Department of Fine Arts/Drama, and he currently maintains involvement in the alumni association. Mielech has enjoyed personal and professional relationships with eight of the college's thirteen presidents and five of its six bishops. A renowned playwright and director, Mielech is a larger-than-life personality and presence around the campus and its alumni.